Original title:
Humor in the Hemlock

Copyright © 2025 Creative Arts Management OÜ
All rights reserved.

Author: Maya Livingston
ISBN HARDBACK: 978-1-80567-333-0
ISBN PAPERBACK: 978-1-80567-632-4

## Satirical Sunlight

Beneath the bright and sunny skies,
The daisies wear their best disguise.
While bunnies dance in comical leaps,
The trees above just shake and weep.

The sun, a jester in a crown,
Spreads warmth while playing pranks in town.
A squirrel slips on a playful nut,
And laughter echoes through the rut.

## Ridiculous Roots

The roots, they giggle underground,
As worms perform a wiggly round.
A cactus wears a silly hat,
And finds it hard to chat with rats.

In every garden, humor blooms,
With veggies shaping funny tunes.
Potatoes sing their tuber songs,
While carrots dance the whole night long.

## **Grins Among the Greenery**

In shrubs and bushes, chuckles rise,
As flowers crack their silly lies.
A beetle dons a shiny tie,
And twirls with pride as passersby.

While daisies tell their finest jokes,
The tulips roll their eyes like folks.
A butterfly's a stand-up star,
In gardens bright, they raise the bar.

## Lighthearted Lament in the Lush

The vines lament in playful rhymes,
Recalling all their silliest times.
With sap that spills like giggling tears,
They sing of hope throughout the years.

Among the ferns, a parrot squawks,
While grasshoppers do funny walks.
Each leaf a tale of laughter spun,
In nature's dance, the jest is won.

## Comedic Crafts in the Canopy

In the treetops, laughter echoes,
Squirrels sporting tiny sombreros.
They juggle acorns, a nutty delight,
While birds chirp jokes, taking flight.

A raccoon wears a bow tie with flair,
Crafting a mask from the soft, cool air.
With giggles and wiggles, the branches sway,
Oh, what a show in the bright ballet!

## Larks Among the Lilacs

Under lilacs, a picnic unfolds,
With ants donning hats and stories told.
A frog plays piano, croaking a tune,
While butterflies dance like a cartoon.

The sandwiches giggle, tickling they seem,
As bees buzz in chorus, fulfilling a dream.
Larks join in, taking a bow,
Oh, if only these moments could last somehow!

## **Peals of Laughter on the Path**

On a winding path where shadows play,
A tortoise jogs in a very slow way.
Snails race past with shells polished bright,
While chipmunks throw seeds, causing a flight.

A hedgehog flips pancakes, a curious sight,
Wobbly dishes take off in delight.
Chasing chuckles through breezy bends,
In this woodland, the laughter never ends!

## Goofy Grove Gatherings

At the grove, strange creatures convene,
Wearing their quirkiest outfits, unseen.
A beaver in boots, a peacock in shades,
All sharing snacks and trade escapades.

They play silly games, tossing their hats,
While raccoons applaud, in striped, fancy flats.
In the sweet sunshine, joy fills the air,
Every moment together, beyond compare!

## The Laughing Leaflet

In a garden where giggles grow,
A leaf wore a grin, to and fro.
Each rustle, a joke to unfold,
With blossoms in laughter, bold.

Squirrels danced under the trees,
Telling tales with the buzzing bees.
A breeze brought a chuckle so bright,
As nature played tricks, pure delight.

The daisies would snicker and sway,
As sunlight painted the day.
Whispers of glee filled the air,
With leaflets that laughed without care.

When twilight crept in with a yawn,
The leaf held its breath, waiting for dawn.
For in the stillness, it knew,
Tomorrow's giggles would bloom anew.

## Gleeful Shadows in a Gloomy Glade

In a shadowy glade where no sun gleamed,
Trees chuckled softly, as if they dreamed.
The darkness with jokes began to play,
Turning gloomy into a lively ballet.

Mushrooms wore hats, colored in jest,
As crickets laughed from their cozy nest.
Even the owl, wise and aloof,
Hooted in rhythm, a comical spoof.

A rabbit hopped past with a wink,
Sipping moonlight, it stopped to think.
With each bound, a laughter arose,
Filling the glade with joy, like prose.

So in the shadows where gloom dared to reign,
The whispers of giggles brought comfort, not pain.
And those who wandered, lost or forlorn,
Found smiles in the night, each dusk reborn.

## Wit Among the Willows

Amidst the willows, with branches so sleek,
A squirrel spun tales, quite quaint and unique.
Each gust of wind was a chuckle so warm,
As twigs intertwined, creating charm.

One willow dipped low, with a playful tease,
"Hey, come tickle my leaves, if you please!"
Below, the pond mirrored laughter's embrace,
Where frogs jumped in for a comedic race.

Old bumblebees buzzed in the air,
Winking at blooms with a debonair flair.
Even the sun, with its golden fit,
Joined in the mirth, casting light on wit.

And at dusk, when the stars dared to peek,
The willows held secrets, giggles to speak.
A tapestry woven of joy and of cheer,
In Nature's own theater, forever near.

# Jests by the Juniper

By the juniper, the laughter takes flight,
With giggles trapped in the cozy twilight.
Squirrels chattered, sharing their roguish tales,
While shadows played tag, tripping on trails.

The spicy scent mingled with moments of glee,
As rabbits danced 'round hummingbirds, carefree.
The juniper waved with a mischievous grin,
Inviting all creatures to join in the spin.

Frogs, in a chorus, croaked out a jest,
While fireflies twinkled, adorning their fest.
The night wore a cloak woven from delight,
With a sprinkle of giggles, under the moonlight.

So listen closely, beneath the stars' gleam,
For laughter resides in each breath, each dream.
In the shade of the juniper, joy finds a way,
To keep all the worries and troubles at bay.

## Amusement Amongst Ashes

In a forest where shadows play,
The trees engage in a silly fray.
A raccoon dons a top hat flair,
While squirrels giggle without a care.

A wise old owl sides with the jest,
Reminding all to laugh their best.
With each crackle of fallen leaves,
They dance around like playful thieves.

Below the boughs, a boot falls flat,
A startled deer jumps, where's her hat!
The brook chuckles as it flows,
Echoing laughter, how it goes!

Even the ashes wear a grin,
Twirling notes of laughter within.
In this realm of cheeky cheer,
Joy echoes loud, resounding near.

## Jestful Jamboree

Beneath the canopy's favorite shade,
Frogs in ties are ready to parade.
A mischievous fox cracks a joke,
While rabbits dance, oh what a stroke!

The marigolds wink in delight,
As raccoons waltz into the night.
A butterfly flutters with flair,
Tickling noses as it darts in air.

Outrageous whispers fill the breeze,
As the trees sway with utmost ease.
In each cackle, joy reborn,
A festival where laughter's worn.

With donuts tossed from lazy clouds,
The critters cheer, they gather crowds.
It's a playful song the forest sings,
Of whimsy and laughter that nature brings.

## **Giggles in the Glade**

In the heart of the wild, what a sight,
Giggling concoctions take off in flight.
Beneath the moon, a dance so bright,
Where shadows prance—a comical rite.

A hen in boots leads a merry chase,
Through fields of daisies, a zany race.
Curly-tailed pigs roll in the mud,
Splashing laughter—a joyful flood.

The owls hoot in rhythmic cheer,
As the crickets chirp, "Come gather near!"
A band of critters, a jolly scene,
With playful puns, a carnival green.

Under the stars, joy swells so wide,
With laughter echoing, hearts open wide.
In the glade, where silliness thrives,
The spirit of fun, forever alive!

## Silliness in the Sylvan

In the sylvan deep where laughter glows,
A turtle prances on its toes.
Birds play tag with the breeze so free,
As pine trees giggle in jubilee.

With every twist, a joke unfolds,
A garden of humor, bold and gold.
A hedgehog jests with a prickly grin,
While the fox rolls back in a fit of spin.

A party unfolds with nutty snacks,
The bunny twirls, while the badger cracks.
Joys abound in this leafy spot,
Forget the worries; let's have a shot!

Under the canopy, smiles ignite,
In this woodland party, every night.
Where silliness soars, and spirits lift,
In the sylvan realm, the heart's best gift.

## **The Comedic Cradle of Nature**

In the garden where daisies dance,
A gnome grins in a silly stance.
The squirrels chuckle at their own play,
As shadows twirl and prance away.

Nature whispers with a gentle tease,
While bumblebees buzz with giggling pleas.
The wind tells jokes in rustling leaves,
And laughter bubbles in the sun's eaves.

Worms serenade in a squishy song,
While ladybugs tag along with a throng.
Each petal's smile, a cheeky jest,
In this cradle, all find their rest.

The stones are wise, yet want to jest,
They hide a joke beneath their crest.
Even the grass looks up and grins,
In this haven, the joy never thins.

## **Snickers from the Soil**

Deep in the earth, secrets hum,
As seedlings giggle, growing dumb.
The roots tap dance, a silent show,
While earthworms twist and slide below.

Mushrooms pop out to poke fun,
As picnic ants march, one by one.
The dirt has tales of mirth to share,
With every laugh, it fills the air.

Frogs croak jokes from their mossy throne,
While crickets chirp, never alone.
Each rustling leaf, a chuckle so sweet,
In the soil's heart, this laughter's treat.

Rocks roll over to join in the jest,
Who knew the ground could be so blessed?
With snickers rising from the deep,
Nature's humor, we gladly reap.

## The Playful Paradox of Pines

Tall pines stand with a wise old grin,
Waving gently in the breeze so thin.
Their needles whisper tales of cheer,
As chipmunks dart, mischief near.

Beneath their branches, shadows play,
A jester's hat for both night and day.
Each gust of wind, a tickling spree,
While pine cones drop, a gift for thee.

Treetops chatter, secrets to spread,
In trunks so stout, humor's wed.
The bark becomes a stage for jest,
In evergreen woods, there's no quest for rest.

Even the sap drips for a laugh,
Silly stories in nature's half.
The playful paradox we embrace,
In this treetop folly, we find our place.

## Chuckling through the Underbrush

In the thicket, laughter creeps,
As hedgehogs roll and the wildflower peeps.
The bushes rustle with a knowing grin,
An unseen jest where chaos begins.

Rabbits leap over roots with glee,
While frogs strike poses—oh, what a spree!
The moonlight tickles the evening air,
As fireflies join in a giggling affair.

Every footprint tells a tale,
Of pranks and jinks on nature's trail.
The leaves rustle with a chuckle bright,
A symphony of joy in the night.

Down low and up high, the laughter weaves,
Through tangled paths where imagination weaves.
In the underbrush, where whispers unite,
The world sings of fun by the pale moonlight.

## Fun in the Fauna

Squirrels chatter with glee,
Dancing on the high tree.
Rabbits hop in a race,
Mischief written on each face.

A fox wears a snarky grin,
Chasing its tail, what a spin!
Birds jest in their sweet song,
Nature laughing all along.

## Lighthearted Leaves

Leaves flutter down with a jig,
Twisting, spinning, oh so big.
The wind whispers, 'Join the fun!'
Nature's party has begun!

Branches sway like silly kids,
Waving arms, no fear or lids.
A joyful rustle in the air,
Laughter echoes everywhere.

## Quips in the Quagmire

A frog croaks a witty line,
While stuck in mud, so divine.
Turtles snicker, slow it seems,
In the mire, they weave their dreams.

Splashing water, a comical sight,
Laughter bounces, pure delight.
The bog's a stage for all to see,
Where even the reeds join in glee.

## Jovial Journeys

A snail boasts of its long trek,
With a wink, it takes a peck.
Crickets chirp, 'What's the rush?'
As they dance and hear the hush.

A butterfly flutters, oh so bright,
'Thankful for every sunny light.'
With giggles shared among the crew,
Their paths are fun, adventures too.

## Merry Melodies Under the Moon

The owls hoot with giggles, so sweet,
Dancing shadows sway on their feet.
Bats in bowties, a sight to behold,
Flapping and flinging, so brash yet bold.

Crickets play tunes with a catchy beat,
While fireflies twinkle, oh what a treat!
Frogs in top hats croak jokes sublime,
Each ribbit a punchline, a rhythm of rhyme.

The moon chuckles softly, a silver delight,
As raccoons debate who has the best bite.
Scraps of old sandwiches tossed in a round,
Result in a feast, laughter's sweet sound.

Under stars that beam with glee and with grace,
Nature's grand concert puts smiles on each face.
In this nocturnal bash, let's dance till the dawn,
For laughter is never finished, just drawn!

## Frivolous Foliage Frolics

Leaves twist and twirl in a playful race,
Caught in the whimsy of nature's embrace.
Squirrels in scarves, what a comical crew,
Chasing their tails without any clue.

Branches do curtsy, swaying with cheer,
Each moment igniting a chuckle or jeer.
Pinecones roll down like clumsy old friends,
Hiding their laughter as mischief transcends.

Dandelions puff with a comical air,
Spreading their seeds like jokes everywhere.
Each gust of wind carries giggles anew,
Tickling the grass where the daisies grew.

In this leafy realm where the fun never fades,
Every rustle and whisper in nature cascades.
The trees wear their smiles, so bright and so bold,
With every frolic, another tale told!

## Hilarious Happenings in the Havens

In the cozy nooks where the wild things play,
Laughter erupts in a boisterous way.
Badgers in slippers, a curious sight,
Rushing through thickets, oh what a delight!

Mice in monocles sip on their tea,
Chortling and chatting, so merrily free.
Giggling toads leap under bright stars,
Crafting their gags with witty repars.

The sun joins the fun with a cheeky grin,
Warming the hearts under skies thick with spin.
Every critter's caper, a comic refrain,
In the havens of joy, there's never a strain.

Branches creak softly with chuckles and cheer,
As nature conspires, its laughter sincere.
Each day's an adventure, a bold escapade,
In this wild, wacky world, where smiles never fade!

## Chuckling Chimes of the Seasons

Winter's frosty breath brings a giggle or two,
Snowmen wobble and dance, dressed in blue.
Ice-skates spin wildly, a slip and a slide,
As laughter erupts from every side.

Spring bursts alive with a playful parade,
Tulips wear hats as they twist and cascade.
Butterflies flutter in skirts made of light,
Painting the garden in colors so bright.

Summer arrives with a sun-drenched cheer,
Picnics and prancing, no worries, no fear.
Lemonade fountains splash joy at each turn,
As giggles parade and the fireflies learn.

Autumn concludes with a rustle and laugh,
Crunching the leaves, nature's joyful gaffe.
Each season a jest, a whimsical spin,
In the chimes of the year, the joy found within!

## Laughter in the Larch

In the shade of twisting limbs,
Silly squirrels make their whims.
Branching out with cheeky flair,
Nutty jokes are in the air.

A wise old owl sings a tune,
Tickling leaves with every croon.
Rabbits hop with playful grace,
Mischief dancing in their pace.

Breezes carry chuckled sound,
Giggling echoes all around.
As shadows play on forest ground,
Joyful pranks are daily found.

Underneath the larch so tall,
Laughter skips and makes us all.
Life's a jest, so why not share,
In the woods, we shed our care.

## Whimsy Beneath the Pines

Beneath the pines, the shadows twist,
Where gnomes and pixies laugh and twist.
Mushrooms wear a cap of jokes,
Giggling softly with the folks.

Whimsical winds pull at the trees,
Bringing laughter with the breeze.
A fox in spectacles looks around,
Finding chuckles on the ground.

Bubbles rise from the brook nearby,
Frogs in bow ties sing, "Oh my!"
With every splash and every croak,
The woods become a stage of folk.

In the dance of shadows bright,
Laughter turns the day to night.
With every leaf that flutters down,
Whimsy reigns, no need to frown.

## Chuckles in the Underbrush

In thick underbrush, the laughter grows,
A tangle of jests where nobody knows.
Critters share tales that twist and twirl,
As flowers giggle and leaves unfurl.

In a thicket, a hedgehog spins,
Telling jokes where the fun begins.
The chatter of crickets fills the night,
With punchlines flying like fireflies bright.

A badger's dance cuts through the mist,
With silly moves that can't be missed.
In every rustle, there's a grin,
Nature's laughter, let's join in!

Under leaves where shadows sway,
Laughter blooms throughout the day.
In the underbrush, life is a jest,
With every giggle, we are blessed.

## Gags Under the Grove

Under the grove, where shadows pool,
A tree stump holds the silliest rule.
With knotted roots and branches wide,
Laughter blooms like flowers beside.

A crow in costume struts around,
Dropping gags from high above ground.
Every quip brings a twinkling eye,
As the wind carries laughter high.

Squirrels toss acorns with a flair,
Creating chaos with every scare.
Their shenanigans are quite the show,
Beneath the grove, the fun will grow.

In the dappled light, joy will thrive,
Every chuckle keeps us alive.
With playful jests from leaf to tree,
In this grove, we're wild and free.

## Smiles Between the Pines

In the shade where shadows play,
Squirrels dance in a quirky way,
Nature chuckles, leaves do sway,
As pinecones drop in a funny fray.

A bear trips over a fallen branch,
Its clumsy slip, a wild romance,
Trees whisper secrets, take a glance,
At all the creatures that dare to prance.

A fox in socks, oh what a sight,
Chasing butterflies with pure delight,
The forest's laughter takes to flight,
Painting the day with colors bright.

Underneath the busy boughs,
Life's a joke that simply allows,
To break from frowns and take a bow,
In this playful world, we make our vows.

## Whimsy Underfoot

Mushrooms giggle in a line,
As ants parade, their steps divine,
The earth below, a jester's mine,
With every root, a twisted vine.

Jumping jacks from sleepy frogs,
Caught in webs spun by tired dogs,
The whimsy here, it plays and clogs,
A dance of life, where laughter smogs.

Curly worms in costumes bright,
Twisting through the soft twilight,
Each wiggle brings a new delight,
In this enchanting, funny night.

Under skies where silliness roams,
Every creature feels like home,
In this land where smiles comb,
Together we are never alone.

## Giggling in the Gloom

In shadows thick, the crickets sing,
While owls vest in wise old bling,
Their silent hoots, a playful fling,
In the dark, bright laughter springs.

A hedgehog sighs, yet rolls with glee,
Leaving trails like confetti spree,
In every corner, joy runs free,
Beneath the watch of a gnarled tree.

Moonlight sparkles on sleepy streams,
As frogs host their zany dreams,
With twinkling stars that burst at seams,
In this merry world of whimsy themes.

Among the gloom, the chuckles rise,
Turning gloom into sweet surprise,
For in the night, laughter defies,
Its magic lingers, never dies.

## Chuckles from the Chasms

Down in the valleys, echoes play,
With every rock in disarray,
The chasms laugh at the light of day,
As shadows stretch in a comical way.

A goat on a ledge, strutting bold,
With a tale that's often retold,
It jumps and hops, no fear of cold,
While laughter bursts like gems of gold.

Rabbits host their silly race,
In a fray of ears, a crowded space,
With giggles weaving, they embrace,
Their frolics crisscross every trace.

In jagged depths where secrets dwell,
A playful spirit weaves its spell,
With every chuckle, all is well,
In nature's heart, we hear the bell.

**Easygoing Echoes in the Understory**

In the shade, the breezes laugh,
While squirrels plot their next big gaffe.
A snail races slow, with style so glum,
But everyone knows he's no quick chum.

A wobbly tower of leaves so high,
Frogs croak jokes as crickets sigh.
The ants march on, a tiny parade,
While a hedgehog rolls, completely dismayed.

Branches sway with giggles unseen,
As flowers gossip, murky and green.
Beneath the fronds, antics unfold,
In a world where silliness is bold.

Echoes of chuckles, soft and bright,
Nature's jesters, a pure delight.
Together they dance in this leafy spree,
Creating smiles for you and me.

## **Jovial Treetop Tales**

High on a branch, the owls convene,
Trading stories so wild and keen.
One tales of a worm who fancied a kite,
As the sun sets low, causing a fright.

Fluffy bunnies join in the fray,
With punchlines that bounce and frolic away.
A raccoon with snacks, a crafty old fool,
Spins yarns of his time in the shiny swimming pool.

A splashing otter, all giggles and grins,
Shares his tales of outsmarting kin.
With fables spun high in the breeze,
Every leaf shakes with laughter, oh please!

When twilight descends, the stars align,
Shimmering bright, like winks divine.
In this grove where joy prevails,
Listen close to the jovial tales.

## Sassy Shadows and Silly Solutions

In the shade, shadows play a game,
While a chameleon's trying to find his name.
A blender of color, a tangle of fun,
But loses his battle with the sun!

A hedgehog wears glasses, what a sight!
Reading the news with absolute delight.
"Why are the bears always so grumpy?" he muses,
"Because they have no time for fun or excuses!"

A wise old turtle speaks with depth,
Making solutions with every breath.
"Why rush through life when you can enjoy?
Pace with the laughter, life should not annoy."

Under the boughs, happenings unfold,
With tricks and quips that can't be controlled.
In the dance of the sassy and silly tonight,
Every heart's light, every soul feels bright.

## **Grins in the Glimmers**

In the morning mist, where dew drops shine,
A fox cracks a joke, feeling divine.
With the sun peeking through the leafy cloak,
Every sprout erupts in laughter, then spoke.

A family of rabbits on a wild hare chase,
Clumsily tumbling, they quicken their pace.
Giggles erupt from under the trees,
As a breeze carries whispers with mischievous tease.

The chipmunk, with acorns, stacks them high,
But tumbles down with a startled cry.
Who knew acorns could be such a mess?
Nature's chuckle is hard to repress.

In the soft glimmers of golden hour light,
Miracles happen, everything feels right.
With each glint and shimmer, the chuckles arise,
Creating the magic that never defies.

# Banter by the Brook

A frog leapt high with a splash of cheer,
Said, "I'd win more races, if not for this sheer!"
The fish just winked, with a glint in his eye,
"You jump and I swim, but who wants to fly?"

The turtle chimed in, with a grin on his face,
"The trick is to slow down, there's no need for haste!"
But the rabbit just laughed, with a twitch of his nose,
"I'll beat you all still, when the hurry up grows!"

The stream gurgled back, with a bubbly delight,
As the sun hung low, painting shadows of light.
Every critter convened, shared a giggle and jest,
In this wacky wild world, they simply felt blessed.

A beeswing came by, with a jig and a buzz,
"Join my happy dance, if you feel you can buzz!"
So they twirled and they stumbled, under branches and leaves,
Creating a ruckus, like playful little thieves.

## Witty Whispers of the Woods

In the depths of the grove, where the shadows converse,
A squirrel spun tales that could fill a whole verse.
"I once stole a pie, fled with no single crumb,
While the baker just scowled, I could hear him say 'Dumb!'"

The owls hooted back with a wise, knowing smirk,
"Young ones, your antics are just how you work!"
With each flap and flap, they spread their good cheer,
Sharing laughter and stories, as night time drew near.

A deer joined the fray, with a playful shy glance,
"Who knew that old trees could hold such a dance?"
And the shadows all chuckled, beneath moon's soft glow,

As they imagined their lives in a wondrous tableau.

A rustle of leaves, as the crickets conspired,
"Let's play hide and seek, in the moonlight we're wired!"

They leapt and they dashed, with giggles that rang,
In the heart of the woods, where the mischief still sang.

# Frolics in the Foliage

Beneath the tall oaks, where the breeze likes to tease,
A chipmunk put on a show, with acorns to seize.
"Watch me juggle!" he cried, with a bright little grin,
But an acorn went flying, and hit him right in!

The vines wrapped around, just to join in the spree,
"We can swing from the branches, or join in a plea!"
A bunny piped up, with a hop towards the sun,
"Who cares who's the best, when we're all having fun?"

The leaves rustled loud, as if laughing in code,
"We'll dance like the shadows, in our leafy abode!"
So twirling and swirling, through the night's gentle calm,
Every creature together, like a fanciful psalm.

As dawn peeked in, with a soft, rosy light,
The frolics subsided, just a hint of delight.
With a grin still intact, they all bid a farewell,
For tomorrow, they'd gather, in the sweet forest dell.

## Jest and Jesticle Amidst the Boughs

In the dappled sunlight, the chatter was loud,
A mockingbird practiced, drawing quite the crowd.
"Watch me mimic a cat!" he crowed with delight,
Only to earn scowls from a nearby old sprite.

A mischievous raccoon, with a wink and a laugh,
Said, "I'd steal your snacks, but I'd rather just daft!"
With a shimmy and shake, he did a silly jig,
And all in the boughs could only laugh big.

The critters together shared pranks, pokes, and glee,
Each jest more absurd than the last one could be.
From the branches fell jokes, like ripe fruit in the fall,
Echoing through thickets, a sweet, merry call.

As the sun dipped low, shadows began to blend,
With hearts full of laughter, it felt like a trend.
So they vowed for tomorrow, more fun to invent,
In their jolly domain, where each jest was meant.

## **Cheeky Chortles at the Campfire**

The campfire crackles, full of cheer,
Marshmallows dance, the jokes come near.
A squirrel juggles nuts with flair,
While shadows wiggle, bursting with air.

Ghost stories told with a giggle or two,
The punchline lurking, but where, who knew?
A raccoon snickers, hiding in a sack,
As laughter echoes, we lose track of snack.

The stars above wink with a grin,
As we roast our laughs, the night wears thin.
Campfire singalongs, voices bold,
Frogs hop by, joining the fold.

So tell me again how the chicken flew,
Between the trees dancing, just like you.
With every chuckle, the night gets bright,
Cheeky chortles make everything right.

# **Laughing Leaves and Loquacious Roots**

Leaves rustle softly, a giggle ensues,
The roots chuckle tales, ancient yet new.
A tree trunk tells jokes, you're in for a treat,
With every bark and bounce, laughter's sweet.

Under the canopy where whispers collide,
The wind carries laughter, a joyous ride.
In every crevice, a pun finds its way,
As branches sway, it's a playful ballet.

Come join the dance, in this leafy embrace,
With roots twisting humor in nature's great space.
Each chuckle ignites the very ground's quirk,
Where laughter blooms, don't you dare lurk!

As shadows stretch long, evening draws near,
The laughter of leaves, a comforting cheer.
With every cackle, the forest awakes,
Loquacious roots whisper, wherever it takes.

## **Ridiculous Riffs in the Rain**

Puddles giggle as raindrops fall,
Each splash a jest, the weather's call.
Umbrellas flip, launching into the air,
While frogs in galoshes hop without a care.

The sky starts to chuckle, clouds play coy,
As umbrellas dance, a parade of joy.
Silly hats float by, like paper boats,
With thunderous laughter from giggling goats.

Raincoats swirl, colors shining bright,
As we stomp in puddles, a joyful sight.
Slippery sidewalks, the comic's flair,
With every slip, we're light as air.

So grab your friends and dance in delight,
These ridiculous riffs make everything right.
With every downpour, we find a new song,
In the rain, dear friend, we truly belong.

## Whimsical Winks in the Wilderness

In the heart of the woods, where shadows play,
The critters converge in a humorous way.
A fox with a hat makes a humorous bow,
While a bird recites sonnets, we wonder how.

The mushrooms giggle, all spots and flair,
As squirrels spin tales in the crisp, cool air.
A raccoon drummed a beat on a tin can,
The laughter cascades, as bright as a fan.

Under the canopy, secrets are spun,
With winks and laughs, the day's just begun.
A deer joins in, stepping to the groove,
In this whimsical world, we begin to move.

So come take a seat on the mossy green floor,
With laughter aplenty, there's always more.
In the wilderness' heart, such joy to unveil,
With whimsical winks, life's a funny tale.

## Chucking in the Canopy

In the treetops, whispers flow,
Squirrels trade jokes, doing a show.
The owls roll their eyes with flair,
While woodpeckers tap out their snare.

Leaves are giggling in the breeze,
Branches sway like dancing knees.
A raccoon snickers, hiding his stash,
As the sunlight begins to splash.

Crickets chirp their silly tunes,
Beneath the watch of crescent moons.
Jokes bounce high from ground to sky,
Nature's laughter soaring by.

So come now, join the leafy laugh,
In this secret, green-lined path.
The canopy's a jolly sight,
Fun and frolic take their flight.

## Frolics in the Ferns

Frogs with hats and polka dots,
Jumping high in silly spots.
Their croaks sound like a joyous tune,
As they dance beneath the moon.

Ferns are swaying, laughing loud,
Tickling toes of passing crowd.
A bunny hops with a cheeky grin,
Joined by beetles, wearing tin.

Tails are wagging, smiles wide,
In the ferns where games abide.
A playful breeze, a tickling touch,
Nature's joy, it means so much.

Come delight in this green embrace,
Where every leaf has a funny face.
With frolics bright, let's sway and twirl,
In the ferns, let laughter unfurl!

## **Cheerful Canopies**

Up above, the sky's a jest,
Every branch a laughing guest.
Sunlight winks through emerald leaves,
While shadows dance and the humor weaves.

Chirping birds, they crack a line,
Jokes exchanged, oh, how they shine!
In cheerful canopies, mirth finds way,
As breezes giggle, come what may.

A chattering chipmunk passes through,
Winking at squirrels, it's all for you.
With every rustle, joy is found,
In hearty laughter, we are bound.

So up above your cares release,
In the tops where laughter's peace.
Join the woodland's jolly crew,
Under cheerful skies so blue!

## Puns in the Pines

In the pines, the whispers swell,
As creatures share their tales to tell.
A porcupine cracks up a rhyme,
In these moments, all feels sublime.

A fox prances, tail held high,
With puns that make the owls fly.
"Oh deer!" they laugh, "What's the score?"
In pinewood shades, we all explore.

Beneath the branches, snickers spread,
Each joke as fresh as forest bread.
Laughter rings from tree to tree,
Join the fun, just you and me.

So tiptoe here with ticklish feet,
Where laughter and the pines do meet.
In every quip, we find delight,
A playful chorus through the night.

## Smirks and Spruce

Beneath the branches, shadows play,
A squirrel prances, bright and gay.
It drops a pinecone, thump and roll,
While birds just chuckle, laugh and stroll.

A fox in a hat, quite out of place,
Tips it at mice in a merry chase.
They dart around, a lively spree,
As chipmunks giggle from their tree.

The mossy ground, a green delight,
Where laughter blooms in soft sunlight.
A rabbit hops, a dance so free,
It twirls and turns with glee, oh me!

The forest whispers silly jokes,
Where even the mushrooms grin like folks.
In every nook, there's jest and cheer,
In the realm of woods, who would fear?

## Merry Mischief Among the Moss

In a patch of moss, so soft and bright,
Frogs wear crowns and jump with might.
They croak a tune, a jolly song,
While beetles march along, so strong.

A hedgehog dons a tiny shoe,
With pirouettes, it twirls anew.
The other critters clap and shout,
As laughter dances all about.

Behind the trees, a prankster's glee,
A raccoon hides, as sly as can be.
With his masked face, he pulls a trick,
As giggles echo, quick and slick.

In every glade, a jest unfolds,
Where tales of laughter are often told.
Among the greens, they play and tease,
In merry mischief, hearts find ease.

# Chortles in the Clearing

In the clearing where the sunlight beams,
Chipmunks swap mischievous dreams.
A tale of nuts and hiding spots,
Causes raucous laughter, like funny plots.

Here comes a hedgehog, wobbly and round,
Chasing its lunch that won't be found.
With snickers shared, and squeaks aloud,
This forest stage draws quite a crowd.

A dance emerges, chaotic and wild,
As bunnies hop like a carefree child.
They race and tumble, unafraid to fall,
Echoing chortles that inspire all.

Beneath the oaks, laughter can thrive,
A secret place where spirits jive.
Among the trees, in cheeky cheer,
The joy of life is ever near.

## **Lightness in the Leaf litter**

In the leaf litter where chuckles rise,
Mysteries twinkle in playful eyes.
A snail with swagger, moving slow,
Shares jokes with ants that come and go.

The wind swoops down, a playful tease,
Rustling leaves with a gentle breeze.
While worms wiggle, much to delight,
Their squirming dances glow in the light.

Dancing dandelions sway and spin,
Their laughter twinkles as tales begin.
A wise old owl, with twinkling gaze,
Frames every whim in a funny phrase.

In every rustle, in every sigh,
The forest invites laughter to fly.
With every step upon the ground,
The joy of play is always found.

## Sarcasm Amongst Shrubs

The shrubs chat loud, a witticism spree,
While daisies chuckle, as bright as can be.
"I'm taller than you!" the ferns brag with glee,
As squirrels roll eyes, sipping tea from a tree.

A prickly old bush says, "What's with the hue?"
"They say I'm just green, but I'm feeling quite blue!"
The bees buzz in laughter, they just can't stay still,
With floral punchlines that give quite a thrill.

The shrubs hold their sides, they can't take the heat,
As a gopher stumbles, with multiple feet.
"Can't tell left from right, but I'm fast when I flee!"
Oh, nature's own jesters, just wait for the spree!

As twilight descends, the banter won't cease,
Each leaf starts to chuckle, they find such release.
With whispers of mischief that lilt through the grove,
The shrubs keep the secrets, so slyly they'll rove.

## Playful Petals

In the garden's embrace, laughter takes flight,
With petals that giggle in soft morning light.
"Who wore it best?" cries the tulip so bold,
As the lilac just snickers, in purple and gold.

The peonies prance, wearing crowns made of dew,
While daisies declare, "I'm the fairest, it's true!"
They toss silly jabs, a friendly bouquet,
In a floral debate that brightens the day.

A butterfly flutters, its wings all a-twirl,
"Can you catch me?" it taunts, in the petals they swirl.
With a dash and a laugh, the blossoms unite,
In a playful ballet, delighting the sight.

As the sun starts to set, the petals all sway,
Whispers of joy, in the soft close of day.
Their laughter now echoes through twilight's embrace,
In a garden of giggles, where all find their place.

## Tickles in the Twigs

Deep in the branches, a giggle runs wild,
While twigs twist and dance, like a playful child.
A robin remarks, with a cheeky little jest,
"Who needs a stage? Look! We're all dressed for the fest!"

The breeze joins in, with ticklish little sighs,
As the leaves shimmy down, to the brightening skies.
"Catch me if you can!" the wind teases low,
While the owls roll their eyes, saying, "Oh, what a show!"

Twigs clash and tap in a merry little beat,
As laughter unravels, where the forest meets.
Branches rustle softly, sharing gossip anew,
In the tickles of twigs, where all nature feels true.

As shadows grow long and the stars wink above,
The trees keep on chuckling, full of warmth and love.
In a symphony of giggles, beneath heaven's dome,
The twigs tell their stories, welcoming home.

## Glee at the Gnarled Roots

The roots twist and tangle, a whimsical sight,
As laughter erupts in the soft fading light.
"Who can untie me?" a vine laughs in cheek,
While the mushrooms all chortle, with joy so unique.

A squirrel plays tag, through the gnarled embrace,
It trips on a root, making quite the shameful face.
"Tag! You're it!" boasts a lone little sprout,
As the wise old oak just chuckles about.

The snickers grow louder, as dusk starts to fall,
While the roots share their tales, oh, they're quite the brawl.
"We once knew a tree, who thought he could dance,
But he toppled and tumbled, that was his last chance!"

With glee in the shadows, as stars start to peek,
The roots weave together a humorous streak.
In the cushiony darkness, all chuckles resound,
In the gnarled roots' laughter, pure joy can be found.

## **Laughter Among the Shadows**

In twilight's grip, the jesters play,
With grins so wide that chase gloom away.
They dance and prance, where shadows creep,
Tickling tales that make the night leap.

A fog of giggles fills the air,
As trees lean close, with branches bare.
The owls hoot soft, a clumsy cheer,
As laughter echoes, bright and clear.

Beneath the stars that wink and wink,
They share their jokes with a merry clink.
The moonbeam beams, in fits of glee,
As all unite in raucous spree.

So join the fun, dismiss the frown,
In shadows where the laughter's crown.
For in this grove, the night's alive,
With every chuckle, we surely thrive.

## Chortles in the Thicket

In tangled leaves, the giggles grow,
A secret world where laughter flows.
The bushes shake with snickers bright,
As creatures plot their silly plight.

A squirrel dons a tiny hat,
And trips on roots, the clumsy brat.
Beneath the boughs, the frogs play chess,
With ribbits that leave all in jest.

A hedgehog sings a cheeky song,
While fireflies flash the night along.
The thicket shakes with merry cheer,
As every whisper draws us near.

So let the night embrace our glee,
With chortles shared so carelessly.
In leafy laughter, we find our way,
Through thickets bright, till break of day.

## The Jester's Grove

In a grove where jesters spin their tales,
They laugh and leap as mischief prevails.
With painted faces, they twist and twirl,
A circus of chaos in an emerald swirl.

A rabbit juggles fruits of gold,
While whispers of giggles, the trees uphold.
A raccoon tumbles down a slide,
As giggles erupt, they cannot hide.

The brook joins in with a playful splash,
As all the critters begin to dash.
With every heartbeat, the joys ignite,
In the jester's grove, all feels just right.

So skip along this vibrant trace,
Where laughter blooms in every space.
For in this land where clowns convene,
Life's richest joy can be seen.

## Mirth Beneath the Canopy

Beneath the leaves, where whispers play,
Mirth spills out in a bright display.
With squirrels cracking jokes in glee,
And shadows dancing, wild and free.

The branches sway with laughter's tune,
As flowers giggle at the moon.
The wind carries jests, light as air,
Embracing all, a spirited affair.

In every nook, the smiles grow wide,
With undersized mice now on the ride.
Through laughter's path, we wander far,
As joy's bright lanterns dim the stars.

So join the mirth beneath this dome,
In nature's lap, we find our home.
With every chuckle, our hearts align,
In this playful place, forever shine.

## Witty Wildflowers

In a garden where giggles bloom,
Sunflowers wear caps, dispelling gloom.
Daisies spin tales, their petals a swirl,
Beech trees chuckle, leaves start to twirl.

Butterflies dance on a breeze of delight,
Tickled by pollen, they flutter in flight.
Roses tell jokes with thorny wit,
While tulips nod and enjoy every bit.

## Joy in the Journey

On a path where laughter guides each step,
Mud puddles giggle, gleefully kept.
Squirrels play tag, their antics a blast,
Every stumble's a giggle, joy unsurpassed.

Clouds wear a smile, raining some cheer,
As breezes whisper, "Let's not disappear!"
With each twist and turn, surprises unfold,
In this quirky tale, we find joy untold.

## Hilarity in the Hollow

In a cozy nook where shadows play,
Frogs croak punchlines, come what may.
Mice wear top hats, throwing a bash,
With cheese for confetti, they leap in a flash.

Trees throw shade, like wisecracks at noon,
Chirping birds sing a laughable tune.
Even the owls hoot riddles so bright,
In this hollow of giggles, all feels just right.

## Jestful Explorations

Venturing forth on a winding spree,
Finding treasures of giggles, just you and me.
Where rocks play tricks and shadows bemuse,
And every misstep leads to hearty news.

Up hills of chuckles, down valleys of glee,
Every twist brings joy, oh can't you see?
With a map of laughter and a compass of fun,
In jestful explorations, our journey's begun!

## Frothy Fables from the Forest

In the woods where shadows play,
A squirrel juggles acorns all day.
A fox wears a hat, so fine and bright,
While rabbits dance under the moonlight.

The trees giggle as breezes whine,
With whispers of secrets, oh, so divine.
A mushroom giggles, round and red,
While playful pranks fill the forest bed.

An owl jokes with a witty bark,
As fireflies blink, igniting the dark.
The pinecones chuckle, rolling around,
In this fabled space, where laughter is found.

The hedgehog dons glasses, dapper and cool,
Reciting riddles by the old mossy pool.
The laughter echoes, inviting and warm,
In frothy fables, the forest takes form.

## Nonsense Near the Nettle

Beneath the nettles, a duck sings low,
Wearing a bowtie in splendid show.
The bees wear crowns made of gold and fluff,
Pretending they are tough, oh that's enough!

A cricket plays tunes that make you grin,
While worms tap dance, their little skins thin.
With giggles echoing, the flowers sway,
In nonsense realms, where laughter's the way.

The grasshoppers leap, trying to fly,
As faint chuckles float like clouds in the sky.
The nettles hum with a quirk and a twirl,
Crafting jokes that make the world whirl.

A turtle complains as he slips on a snail,
Saying, "Life's too slow, let's set sail!"
In this nutty nook, where the silly abound,
Nonsense mingles with joy all around.

## Amusing Adventures in the Arboretum

In an arboretum, busy and bright,
Trees throw parties that last through the night.
A parrot tells tales, quite tall and absurd,
While wise owls nod, and the bushes confer.

The branches sway with glee and delight,
As squirrels put on a nut-collecting fight.
A flower blushes, its petals unfold,
Sharing secrets that never get old.

The benches complain about weighty affairs,
As ants stage a play with chubby bear stares.
With every giggle, the leaves start to dance,
In this arboretum full of pure chance.

A strange tree whispers riddles with flair,
Sending giggling fawns darting everywhere.
Adventures unfold in this vibrant dream,
Where nature crafts joy, a luminescent beam.

## **Raucous Revelry in the Reed**

In the reedy wilds where the waters weep,
Frogs toss parties that last till sleep.
They wear tiny shoes and fancy socks,
While the dragonflies dance in wild flocks.

The reeds sway and whistle a merry tune,
A bash of laughter beneath the moon.
With puffs of wind, they play hide and seek,
Where giggles burst forth, bold and unique.

A turtle sings with a voice so deep,
Encouraging all to join in the sweep.
While fish splash about, cracking their jokes,
In this raucous realm where delight awoke.

The cattails chuckle as they bend and sway,
Holding secret tales of fun at play.
In the reeds, every creature is a friend,
Sharing laughter and joy that will never end.

## Witty Wanderings in the Woodlands

Amidst the trees, a squirrel danced,
With acorns clutched, it pranced and pranced.
A rabbit laughed, with ears so wide,
He tripped on roots, in glee, he cried.

The owls a-hoo, with wise old eyes,
They whispered tales, spun wild, and sly.
While foxes play, in shadows slight,
Their sneaky games brought pure delight.

Frogs croaked jokes from muddy banks,
While skunks told tales of daring pranks.
Each creature's quip, a playful cheer,
A woodland show, to hold so dear.

So laugh, dear friend, in nature's light,
Where giggles bloom, and spirits ignite.
In every nook, a jest awaits,
The woods alive with laughing fates.

## Radiant Riddles in the Retreat

In the retreat where shadows play,
A gnome told riddles, bright as day.
With misty smiles and twinkling eyes,
He lured us close with cunning lies.

A bird then chirped, a puzzling sound,
And tumbling leaves all danced around.
We scratched our heads and wondered loud,
At clever tricks and laughter proud.

Bunnies hopped, with jokes so spry,
They bounced on clouds, up to the sky.
Each line they tossed, like fairy dust,
In friendly fun, we found our trust.

Amid the trees, where breezes sigh,
The riddles spark, and spirits fly.
So join the jest, and laugh away,
In nature's arms, bright as the day.

## **Jolly Jests Among the Jillingtons**

In Jillington, the laughter flows,
With playful heart, the mischief grows.
A cat in shades grinned wide and bright,
He played a trick on a passing kite.

The townsfolk gathered, brimming with cheer,
As ducks in hats waddled near.
They quacked their lines, both bold and proud,
And filled the air with giggles loud.

A child spills juice, oh what a splash!
The ants march forth, a tiny clash.
With every stumble, every spill,
The jests unfold, a joyful thrill.

So raise a glass, let's toast tonight,
To laughter shared, the world so bright.
In Jillington, we find our song,
With jolly laughs that can't go wrong.

## Whirlwinds of Whimsy in the Wilderness

In wilderness where breezes twirl,
A bear in boots gave quite a whirl.
He danced on logs, a sight so rare,
With every step, he tossed his hair.

The deer joined in, with ballet grace,
Spinning round in a furry race.
While raccoons clapped, their paws in glee,
A merry dance, so wild, so free.

Bubblegum trees burst with delight,
As laughter bubbled, oh what a sight!
A porcupine juggled apples bright,
The whimsy struck, a pure delight.

So let the winds of laughter blow,
In nature's heart, let joy bestow.
With every twist, and every turn,
In the wilderness, our spirits burn.

## Sarcasm Sprouting in the Serenity

In a field of whispers, a sly smile grows,
Where daisies wink and the wisecrack flows.
The sun beams brightly on the laughter's seed,
While shadows dance, fulfilling each need.

There's a frog in a tux, quite out of place,
Croaking with flair, like it's part of the race.
Butterflies gossip, flitting to tease,
While the breeze carries secrets with playful ease.

A squirrel flashes shades, he's got quite the flair,
In a flamboyant top hat, he struts with care.
The trees shake their limbs, tickled by the jest,
Nature's own chorus, it's simply the best.

So take heed of the chuckles, the world's lighthearted song,
In every little quirk, we all belong.
Find joy in the quirks, let the laughter unveil,
In the thicket of life, let your spirit set sail.

## The Quip that Wiggled

A worm in a bowtie, wriggling along,
Sings notes of sarcasm, a wormy tongue throng.
The ants all applaud, with tiny little claps,
As nature's odd humor unfolds with mishaps.

In the meadow where daisies wear crowns made of gold,
A ladybug reigns, with tales to be told.
Each flutter a punchline, each landing a laugh,
Creating a kingdom, a quirky craft.

With a bee as a sidekick, buzzing quite loud,
They craft little stories, enough to make proud.
Their shenanigans rippling through blades of green,
In laughter, they flourish, a sight to be seen.

So join in the fun, let your spirit take flight,
In the wiggle and giggle, find joy day and night.
Every chuckle a journey, every joke a delight,
In this garden of whimsy, everything feels right.

## Amusement in the Undergrowth

Beneath the tall ferns, where shadows play tricks,
A raccoon is plotting, with cunning and flicks.
He juggles bright acorns, quite a sight to behold,
While the owls sit nearby, their wisdom retold.

Crickets compose symphonies, both silly and spry,
As fireflies twinkle, like stars in the sky.
Each giggle of nature, a chorus divine,
In laughter, they weave a whimsical line.

A turtle in slippers, slow but so proud,
Dances a jig, drawing in the crowd.
With shells full of humor, they spin tales of glee,
In the undergrowth's embrace, so wild and free.

So stroll through the underbrush, let laughter ring clear,
In the heart of the forest, find joy without fear.
Every chuckle a treasure, every grin a delight,
In this world of whoppers, the spirit feels light.

## Laughter's Lost Path

In a garden of whimsy, where giggles reside,
The gnomes share secrets, their joy amplified.
With antics and tricks, they dance in the shade,
As flowers burst forth, in colors they've made.

A cat in a bow, speaks wise yet absurd,
With a purr that quips, and laughter's unheard.
On a stroll through the cosmos, quirks come alive,
Leading all wanderers to happily thrive.

Beneath tangled vines, where giggles conspire,
A pot of gold jokes igniting the fire.
Each pun is a pebble along this lost way,
With chuckles to guide, brightening the day.

So follow the path where the goofy reside,
In laughter's embrace, we take each stride.
Through twists and through turns, let joy be our guide,
In this comical journey, where smiles never hide.

## Mirthful Meadows

In fields where daisies dance around,
A goat wears glasses, quite profound.
It reads a book, a curious sight,
While bees do giggle in daylight.

The sun shines bright with cheeky flair,
While rabbits play tag without a care.
A hedgehog sings a silly tune,
Underneath the glowing moon.

The flowers whisper, 'What a day!'
A lark joins in, with much to say.
Each blade of grass is filled with glee,
As laughter spills, wild and free.

Chasing butterflies in silly loops,
Amidst the joy, the meadow troops.
A squirrel dons a tiny hat,
Inviting friends to sit and chat.

## Jocular Woods

In woods where shadows play and creep,
A wise old owl begins to peep.
He cracks a joke about the moon,
Makes all the critters laugh in tune.

The rabbits hop in comic stride,
While foxes sneak and giggle wide.
A turtle tells a silly tale,
Of the day he danced in the gale.

Trees sway gently, tickled by breeze,
As whispers carry through the leaves.
A creaky branch joins with a squeak,
And all the forest starts to geek.

A funny hat on a tiny gnome,
As woodlandfolk feel right at home.
They gather round the old campfire,
Sharing jokes that never tire.

## Banter in the Birch

Underneath the birchy crown,
A mischievous squirrel scampers around.
He plays the flute, then trips on air,
And all the critters stop and stare.

A raccoon adds a snappy beat,
While rabbits tap with furry feet.
Foxes chuckle, rolling in mirth,
This lively scene, a joyous birth.

The wind plays tricks with leaves so bright,
Sending whispers up into twilight.
They laugh at clouds that tumble by,
As giggles float up to the sky.

A sleepy bear joins in the fun,
With dreams of honey and a pun.
Laughter echoes through the night,
In the birch grove, all feels right.

## Smiles in the Shadows

In corners where the shadows play,
A mouse dons shoes to dance away.
With twirls and spins, he takes the stage,
Turning each whisper into a page.

A crafty fox rolls in a ball,
While cozy hedgehogs are having a ball.
The owls hoot in a rhythm so sweet,
As tiny ants tap to their beat.

Moonlight glimmers on grinning beams,
Painting the night with glowing dreams.
All critters join in perfect fair,
Crafting laughter to fill the air.

In cuddly huddles, stories unfold,
Of trickster tales and treasures untold.
With every chuckle, joy gets spread,
In shadows where giggles gently tread.

## Jokes on the Journey

In a forest where the trees sway,
A squirrel spins tales of the day.
With acorns tossed like jokes in flight,
Laughter echoes, pure delight.

A rabbit hops with a hat askew,
A punchline lands, it's all brand new.
The owls giggle, their heads a-twirl,
As leaves dance down, giving a whirl.

The stream gurgles, a chuckle inside,
As fish leap up, with joy they glide.
Each path taken is lined with cheer,
In woodland shadows, we draw near.

So join the parade, let laughter ring,
For nature's jest is a wondrous thing.
With every step, let your heart be light,
In this journey, joy takes flight.

## The Gleeful Grove

In the grove where the sunbeam plays,
Tiny fairies dance in a maze.
Their giggles tinkle like bells in the air,
While branches sway in their whimsical flair.

A bear in boots tries to waltz along,
He trips and tumbles, but carries a song.
The fox in a bowtie offers a jest,
In a furry tux, his spirit is best.

The mushrooms chuckle, their spots a delight,
As critters gather 'neath stars shining bright.
Each breeze carries whispers of fun,
In a woodland where laughter is never done.

So come join the fun, lose track of time,
In the gleeful grove, joy turns to rhyme.
Each moment is magic, each heart beats bold,
In this merry wood, let happiness unfold.

## Smirk from the Soil

Deep in the earth, where the worms wiggle,
Buried secrets make the flowers giggle.
Each root whispers tales of cheer,
As soil smirks with stories to share.

The carrots tease as they peek from below,
While radishes blush in the garden's glow.
The turnips chuckle with leafy hats,
As nature crafts laughter, soft as spats.

Rain drops chuckling like little pearls,
Splashing on veggies, giving twirls.
And as the sun stretches its rays so wide,
The garden blooms with joy inside.

Let's relish the fun that nature brings,
In each sprout, you'll find what laughter sings.
With every harvest, a grin anew,
The soil's embrace, where smiles break through.

## Woodland Wits

In the woods where the wise ones play,
Mice in glasses hold court all day.
With quips and puns, they spin the yarn,
Creating laughter from dusk till dawn.

A hedgehog reads from a thistle's spine,
While rabbits nod, declaring it fine.
The raccoons clink acorns like merry cups,
As they toast to the night and all that's up.

The fireflies blink with a comic spark,
In the heart of the trees, we light our park.
Each rustle a chuckle in the night air,
Where woodland wits craft joy beyond compare.

So gather 'round, let the stories flow,
In this woodland of laughter, let's steal the show.
For every twist in the tale we weave,
Brings smiles and cheer, and we all believe.

## **Giddy Gatherings at the Grotto**

Under the rocks, where shadows play,
Giggling whispers, come what may.
Frogs wear hats, and crickets sing,
In this spot, joy is the king.

Friends in chaos, laughter flows,
Tumbling tales, the joy that grows.
Bubbles rising from the stream,
Here, the wildest dreams take gleam.

A squirrel jokes, a bird takes flight,
Dancing shadows in fading light.
Jests float like leaves on the breeze,
In this grotto, all at ease.

Chasing echoes of our cheer,
Every moment holds so dear.
With silly games and playful pranks,
Together, we pull off the ranks.

## **Lively Laughs by the Lake**

Ripples sparkle, spin and sway,
Tickling toes, where children play.
Splashy jumps and goofy dives,
In our hearts, spirit thrives.

With ducks in bow ties, smiling wide,
Belly laughs we cannot hide.
Wobbly boats and rowdy cheers,
Banishing all of our fears.

A fish with jokes swims near the shore,
Each new tale leaves us wanting more.
Under sun's warm, playful beam,
By the lake, life's a dream.

Within this glee, we dance and sing,
Joyful hearts, in seasons bring.
Moments stitched with love and mirth,
Embrace the joy of our shared earth.

## Amusing Antics Under the Arbor

Beneath the leaves so thick and green,
Where giggles float, and sights are seen.
Cats wear shades, and mice do prance,
In the shadows, all take a chance.

With whispers soft and crazy winks,
Nature's punchlines, oh how it links!
Twisted vines, a jolly crew,
Spinning tales, both old and new.

In our hideaway, secrets lie,
With silly dances, we reach the sky.
Each chuckle, brighter than the last,
Here, our worries fade so fast.

As the sun sets, bright hues ignite,
Stories weave into the night.
Our laughter echoes like a song,
Under the arbor, where we belong.

## Whimsies of the Wildflower Way

Dancing petals in the breeze,
Bumblebees with funky knees.
Every bloom has tales to share,
Laughter blooms without a care.

Mice in slippers, ants in line,
Telling stories, oh so fine.
Wobbling daisies, green and bold,
In this place, we break the mold.

A wandering goat, wearing a crown,
Joins our revels, never a frown.
With each blossom, whimsy grows,
In our hearts, pure joy flows.

Along this path, we twirl and sway,
Catching giggles at the end of the day.
In wildflower fields, we find our way,
Living life in a bright display.

www.ingramcontent.com/pod-product-compliance
Lightning Source LLC
Chambersburg PA
CBHW051630160426
43209CB00004B/581